BREAKING UP WITH YOUR PHONE

Tips For A Restful Night

Mercy Lawrence

Table of Contents

INTRODUCTION

Why We Need to Reclaim Our Nights

Imagine winding down at night, free from the glow of screens, feeling truly ready for sleep. For most of us, this kind of night time peace seems like a luxury or even an impossible goal. Our phones, tablets, and other screens have become constant companions, not just tools for productivity or connection.

They are often the last thing we see before closing our eyes, and they play a powerful role in shaping how well—or poorly—we rest.

This book is about taking back our nights, reclaiming time for ourselves, and creating habits that support real rest.

By understanding how screens impact our natural rhythms, we can make simple, meaningful changes that lead to a calmer mind, better sleep, and a refreshed start each morning. Reclaiming your nights isn't just about sleeping better; it's about creating more energy, clarity, and space for the things that make life feel vibrant and fulfilling.

The Science of Screens and Sleep Disruption

Most people know that screen time can make it hard to sleep, but understanding the science behind it reveals how deeply our devices influence us.

Each evening, our brains release melatonin, which signals it's time to wind down. But the blue light from screens disrupts this natural rhythm by mimicking daylight.

When you're on your phone late at night, it delays melatonin release, keeping your brain alert and pushing back the time you naturally fall asleep.

Then there's the psychological pull—whether it's one more episode, a quick scroll through messages, or checking tomorrow's weather. This constant engagement keeps the mind active, preventing the wind-down period essential for restful sleep. Studies have shown that late-night screen use can lead to "social jetlag," in which our internal clocks are out of sync, leading to tired, foggy mornings.

By tuning into this science, we can see why swapping screen time for quiet, mindful routines before bed can help our bodies settle into sleep naturally. This knowledge empowers us to make choices that align with our body's natural rhythms, setting the stage for genuine rest.

A Roadmap for Transformation: Breaking Up with Your Phone

Changing your relationship with your phone doesn't mean abandoning it altogether; it means building habits that let you control your device rather than letting it control you. Throughout this book, you'll find practical tools, nightly routines, and mindset shifts designed to create more phone-free time and allow you to sleep deeply. This approach is about small changes that add up, guiding you toward a healthier relationship with technology without sacrificing smartphones' connectivity or convenience.

Each step in this journey offers actionable strategies that fit into real life, helping you gradually reduce night time screen time in a natural and achievable way. This roadmap empowers you to protect your nights from digital interruptions, creating space for the kind of sleep that truly recharges you. Reclaiming your nights isn't just a one-time goal; it's a lifelong practice that will open the door to better sleep, brighter mornings, and a renewed sense of calm.

Chapter 1

The Modern Sleep Crisis

The Cost of Staying Connected: Mental and Physical Toll

Today, daytime activity and night time rest have blurred in today's hyper-connected world. Many people find themselves scrolling through news feeds or checking messages even as they lie in bed, hoping to unwind. But instead of relaxation, these habits create a cycle of heightened alertness and stress.

Our bodies are not built to stay "n" around the clock, and the mental strain of constant connection takes a toll on our minds and bodies. Studies show that staying connected late into the night leads to fragmented sleep and prolonged fatigue. The barrage of notifications and updates mentally keeps our brains engaged, often stirring up anxiety or a sense of "feeding" to stay updated.

This constant vigilance makes it difficult for our minds to wind down at night, keeping stress hormones like cortisol elevated. Physically, this disruption affects everything from immunity to heart health. Lack of quality sleep is linked to inflammation, increased stress levels, and even a greater risk of chronic illnesses over time.

The answer isn't a complete disconnect but creating intentional boundaries around tech use. By gradually reducing screen time in the evenings, you allow your mind to disengage from the digital world, making room for restful sleep.

Letting go of the need to stay constantly connected doesn't mean missing out—it's an investment in your health, helping you feel more focused, calm, and recharged each morning.
Blue Light and Its Effects on Your Sleep Cycle

Blue light—the wavelength of light emitted from screens—significantly impacts our sleep cycles or circadian rhythms. This rhythm acts like an internal clock, telling us when to wake up, eat, and, most importantly, sleep. Natural sunlight contains blue light, which helps regulate wakefulness. But when we expose ourselves to blue light after dark, it disrupts this natural rhythm.

Imagine you're lying in bed, browsing on your phone or tablet. The blue light from these devices mimics daylight, signalling to your brain that it's still daytime.

As a result, the brain suppresses melatonin, the hormone responsible for sleepiness, making it harder to fall asleep and reducing your sleep quality. This interference can lead to irregular sleep patterns, which affects energy levels, mood, and cognitive function the next day.

To minimize blue light exposure, consider using a digital curfew, where screens are turned off an hour or more before bed. Alternatively, using blue-light-blocking glasses or activating the "night mode" feature on devices can lessen the impact.

The goal is to align our evening routine with natural cues for sleep, giving our brains the message that it's time to wind down. Small changes like dimming lights in the evening, swapping screen time for a book, or relaxing music can set you up for a restful night.

The Social Media Trap: How Apps Keep Us Hooked

Social media is designed to engage and retain our attention. Features like infinite Scrolling, personalized feeds, and notification alerts are carefully crafted to encourage us to stay on our phones longer than we might intend. The effects can be addictive, leading to cycles of compulsive checking that interfere with sleep and overall well-being.

Whenever we get a "like," comment, or new follower notification, our brain releases a small amount of dopamine, the neurotransmitter associated with pleasure and reward. This process is similar to what happens with other addictive activities, creating a feedback loop that keeps us coming back for more.

Social media is particularly enticing at night when we feel relaxed and may crave entertainment. But instead of winding down, we're stimulating our brains, making it difficult to let go and sleep.

Setting limits on social media use can free up time and mental space. Try setting your phone to "Not Disturb" mode an hour before bed or moving social media apps to a less accessible location on your device.

Building intentional habits around social media use, like restricting it to certain times of the day, can help you stay in control, protecting your mental health and sleep.

Unmasking Digital Addiction

Digital addiction might sound like a strong term, but many people experience some level of dependency on their devices.

This dependence is not limited to phones or social media; it includes any screen-related habit that interferes with daily life, work, or sleep. Digital addiction is often the result of habitual behaviors reinforced over time, like checking notifications the moment they appear or using devices to cope with stress and boredom.

Spotting the Signs of Phone Dependence

Recognizing phone dependence is the first step toward reclaiming control over digital habits. Some common signs include:

Phantom Notifications: Do you ever "feel" your phone vibrate only to find no notification? This phenomenon is common among those who check their phones habitually. A sign that the mind has become conditioned to expect constant engagement.

Compulsive Checking: You may notice yourself checking your phone even when there's a need—like during conversations, meals, or late at night. Compulsive checking can interfere with real-life connections and prevent you from being fully present.

Anxiety When Separated from the Phone: If the thought of being without your phone makes you feel anxious or uncomfortable, it could be a sign of dependence. This sense of "feeding" the device results from habits formed over time, creating a reliance on digital engagement.

By identifying these habits, you can address and reduce them, creating boundaries that support better sleep and a balanced relationship with technology.

The Cycle of Dopamine: Why You Keep Reaching for Your Phone

Dopamine, often called the "eel-good" chemical, plays a central role in phone dependence. Your brain releases dopamine whenever you receive a notification, message, or social media interaction. This creates a feedback loop that reinforces the habit of checking your phone, even without a conscious need or desire.

Imagine each notification as a mini-reward. The brain craves this reward, making it difficult to resist checking.

Over time, the brain starts associating phone use with positive reinforcement, so reaching for your device during any free moment can feel almost automatic.

The cycle can become even more ingrained when phone use becomes a coping mechanism for stress or boredom, with dopamine acting as the reward.

Breaking this cycle is challenging, but it's possible. One approach is introducing mindful practices, like taking a deep breath before reaching for the phone or setting intentional times for checking messages and notifications.

By becoming more aware of why we get our phones, we can break the habit, creating space for other rewarding activities that support rest.

Myth-Busting: Common Misconceptions About Phone Usage and Sleep

Many people believe they can balance screen time and sleep, often falling into common myths that can undermine sleep quality. Here are a few of those misconceptions and the truth behind them:

Myth: "Just Need to Lower the Brightness" While reducing brightness can lessen eye strain, it doesn't eliminate blue light or prevent overstimulation. Blue light-blocking glasses or night mode are better options, but a break from screens is ideally best for sleep.

Myth: "Scrolling Helps Me Unwind" "Scrolling might feel relaxing, but a form of engagement that keeps the mind alert. Instead of truly winding down, the brain is stimulated by content, which can delay sleep onset. Replacing scrolling with activities like reading a book or meditative breathing can foster relaxation without digital stimulation.

Myth: "I "Just Check One Last Time." "The "one last check" mentality often leads to prolonged phone use as new notifications or updates pull you in. This habit can disrupt your intention to sleep, turning what should have been a quick check into an extended distraction. Setting boundaries, like " no phone after 9 p.m.," "can help create a more predictable routine.

Myth: "Need My Phone to Fall Asleep" "Many people believe they need a phone for soothing activities like listening to music or white noise. While sound can be helpful for sleep, devices can bring added temptations. Consider non-digital options like a white noise machine or present playlists, allowing you to enjoy soothing sounds without the temptation of screen time.

NOTE

In the digital age, it's easy to fall into habits that disrupt sleep. From blue light exposure to social media, modern technology creates unique challenges to maintaining healthy sleep routines. But by recognizing these patterns and making small changes, we can regain control of our night time routines, improve sleep quality, and set ourselves up for a healthier, more energized life.

Chapter 2

Preparing to Break Up with Your Phone

Mindset Shifts for Success

Breaking free from night time phone habits starts with setting your mind to it. Each small step you take toward better sleep is a move toward overall well-being, and it's a journey that requires a clear focus and commitment. The following sections provide a roadmap to shift your mindset, create motivation, and set up your surroundings for better rest.

Visualizing a Restful Night: Why It's Worth It

Imagine waking up feeling really refreshed—no lingering tiredness, no grogginess, just genuine restfulness that carries you through the day. This is what a restful night can provide, and it begins with a commitment to a screen-free sleep routine. Visualizing the benefits of this change can serve as powerful motivation.

Close your eyes and picture the effects: brighter mornings, sharper focus, more stable energy levels, and even improved mood.

A restful night's sleep means your mind has a chance to clear out the mental clutter that builds up during the day. This cleansing process impacts how you process memories, emotions, and thoughts.

As you visualize, consider how clear-headedness, calmness, and resilience can enrich your daily life. Think of this goal as an upgrade to the quality of your day-to-day life—an investment that makes each day a little bit better.

Building Motivation: A Reward System for Good Sleep

Motivation is the driving force that turns intentions into actions, and building a reward system can keep you on track. Rewarding yourself doesn't have to be complex; even small, meaningful rewards can help cement this new habit.

Start with weekly rewards. For instance, if you put your phone away an hour before bed every night for a week, treat yourself to a small luxury: a relaxing bath, a new book, or a favorite snack.

Make your reward system gradual and build it around consistency. Set monthly rewards for sustaining the habit—such as trying out a new café over the weekend, buying that cozy blanket you've had your eye on, or spending a quiet morning without screens.

When you can look forward to rewards emphasizing rest, it reinforces the concept of screen-free sleep as a positive experience. By connecting putting your phone down to the feeling of treating yourself well, you build a feedback loop that encourages better habits.

Recognizing Triggers and Replacing Habits

The reasons we reach for our phones before bed often have little to do with the phone itself; instead, they stem from underlying habits, stress, or boredom. Identifying the "why" behind the habit is essential to replacing it with something healthier.

Start by observing your routine. Are you scrolling because you're anxious or simply because you're looking to unwind? There may be a particular app you go to when you're feeling restless. Each trigger allows you to replace that urge with an activity that addresses your needs.

For example, if you're winding down from a busy day and find it hard to detach, try a short meditation or deep breathing exercise before bed. If you're tempted to open social media out of habit, keep a book or journal within reach. Experiment with alternatives and focus on how these changes make you feel.

By intentionally replacing screen time with fulfilling activities, you create a bedtime routine that meets your needs for relaxation, calm, and self-care.

Setting the Stage: Phone-Free Sleep Spaces

Creating a space that encourages rest is key to helping you commit to screen-free nights. Your sleep environment can be a powerful tool in supporting your goal; small changes can make a big difference.

When your surroundings are designed for rest, it's easier to let go of your phone and lean into comfort and relaxation.

Designing a Bedroom Sanctuary

Think of your bedroom as a personal haven where the only objective is rest. When the room's design reflects that purpose, your mind associates it with relaxation. Start by considering the layout and decor. Declutter surfaces to minimize distractions, making your space feel open and calming. Add elements that make you feel comfortable and cozy, like soft bedding, pillows, or a warm throw blanket.

When choosing colors, lean toward soft, neutral tones that promote relaxation, like muted blues, greys, or warm earth tones. Add small, personal touches—a framed photo, a small plant, or artwork that brings you joy.

When you step into a space that feels truly yours and radiates calm, it becomes easier to let go of digital distractions and allow your body to unwind.

Tech-Free Zones: The Importance of Physical Boundaries

Creating physical boundaries between yourself and your phone is a practical way to reduce the temptation to check it. Start by designating your bed as a tech-free zone. This simple rule keeps your bed associated only with sleep, helping your brain shift more easily into rest mode.

Place your phone somewhere out of reach, like on a dresser or nightstand across the room. This approach does two things: it prevents you from mindlessly picking up your phone before sleep and keeps the room's focal point—your bed—dedicated solely to rest.

Consider investing in a traditional alarm clock if you use your phone as an alarm. This change can be transformative, helping you avoid the "just one more scroll" habit.

Creating a tech-free zone can also mean setting boundaries in other areas of the house, such as a specific chair or nook where you can enjoy screen-free time before bed. This separate space becomes a reminder to unwind, making it easier to let go of screens and relax in the hour before bedtime.

Using Lighting, Sound, and Scents to Signal Rest

Your senses play a significant role in helping your body wind down. By adjusting lighting, adding soothing sounds, and incorporating calming scents, you can signal to your brain that it's time to relax and prepare for sleep.

Lighting: Opt for warm, soft lighting in your bedroom, which promotes a sense of calm. Consider dimmable lamps or even a bedside lantern with a soft glow to reduce stimulation.

Avoid harsh overhead lighting and gradually lower lights as bedtime approaches. This practice mimics natural sunset light, signalling your body that it's time to wind down.

Sound: If background noise helps you sleep, try a white noise machine or nature sounds. Gentle sounds like rainfall, ocean waves, or soft winds can mask external noise and create a peaceful environment. Soft, instrumental music, especially without lyrics, can be a pleasant way to relax without engaging your brain too actively.

Scent: Aromatherapy can be a powerful tool for bedtime relaxation. Scents like lavender, chamomile, and cedarwood are known for their calming properties.

You can add a few drops of essential oil to a diffuser, spray your pillow with a sleep mist, or light a candle (blowing it out before you settle in).

Incorporating scent into your sleep routine can help cure your brain that it's time for rest, making it easier to let go of the day's stress and phone distractions.

Pulling It All Together: The Power of Consistency

Building new habits takes time, and the key to success lies in consistency. Remember to be patient with yourself as you begin to apply these mindset shifts, rewards, and sleep-space changes. Each night you commit to a phone-free evening is a win, and the positive changes will add up over time.

Notice how these practices impact your nights and your entire day. With each small step, you're paving the way to a restful night and a more balanced approach to technology, creating a future where quality sleep becomes the norm rather than the exception.

Chapter 3

The Digital Detox Plan

Crafting a Bedtime Routine That Sticks

Creating a pre-sleep routine can be as simple as weaving together a few calming practices that feel natural and enjoyable. You're signaling to your mind and body that it's time to unwind. Here's how you can ease into the evening:

Choose Calming Activities

Swap out phone time with simple activities that leave you feeling calm. It could be as basic as reading a physical book, doing light stretches, or spending a few minutes journaling. The goal is to ease yourself into rest without overwhelming your senses.

Keep It Consistent

Consistency is key. Try starting and ending your evening routine around the same time each night. Your body will start associating these cues with sleep, making it easier to wind down.

Use Lighting to Set the Mood

Dim lights, or even candlelight, can help prepare your body for rest by signalling that it's night. Consider keeping screens and bright lights out of your bedroom, making it a calming, tech-free zone.

Steps to Replace Scrolling with Soothing Activities

Here are a few practical activities you can try instead of scrolling:

Gentle Stretching

Even five minutes of gentle stretching can release tension and prepare your body for rest. Focus on areas where you typically hold stress, like your neck and shoulders.

Breathing Exercises

Try a simple breathing exercise like inhaling deeply, holding for a few seconds, and then exhaling slowly. This naturally calms the nervous system, helping you feel centered and ready for bed.

Listen to Calming Sounds

Nature sounds, calming music, or audiobooks can be a good alternative to screen time. Set a timer if you're worried about falling asleep with it on, or try listening for just a few minutes to help you unwind.

Journaling or Reading

Reflecting on the day or reading a few pages of a book (ideally not on a screen) can be deeply relaxing. Try focusing on light or positive topics to keep your mind at ease.

A Simple Guide to Meditation for Beginners

Meditation is a powerful tool, especially for unwinding at night. You don't need to make it complicated—just a few minutes of focus can help you let go of the day. Here's a beginner-friendly approach:

Find a Comfortable Position

Sit or lie down in a position that feels good. Close your eyes and take a few slow breaths to relax your body.

Focus on Your Breath

Notice each inhale and exhale. If your mind wanders, gently bring your focus back to your breathing. Try counting each breath if it helps you stay present.

Let Thoughts Come and Go

Your mind will likely drift, and that's perfectly okay. Instead of fighting it, notice your thoughts without holding onto them. Think of them as clouds passing by—acknowledge and let them float away.

Ease Out Gently

When you're ready, slowly open your eyes. Take a moment to notice how you feel, then continue your evening.

Night-by-Night: A 30-Day Detox Plan

Week 1: Reducing Screen Time and Setting Boundaries

Goal: Start by cutting back on screen time a little each night. Begin by putting your phone away 10-15 minutes earlier than usual.

Tip: Use this extra time to try one of the relaxing activities listed above. Reflect on any changes you notice in your sleep or mood.

Week 2: Replacing Digital Habits with Relaxing Rituals

Goal: Use the time you've gained from reduced screen time to build up your new bedtime rituals. Try at least one calming activity each night to ease into sleep.

Tip: Experiment with stretching, reading, or journaling activities to see what works best. This is your chance to create a ritual that feels personal and rewarding.

Week 3: Phone-Free Evenings: Establishing New Patterns
Goal: Try to make your evenings screen-free altogether. This week, aim to turn off screens an

hour before bed. Create a routine that feels comfortable and consistent.

Tip: If an hour feels like too much, ease into it. Adjust based on what feels manageable, but prioritize calming activities instead of screens.

Week 4: Staying Consistent and Tracking Your Progress

Goal: Reflect on your progress and adjust as needed. Continue your screen-free evenings and review what has worked well in your routine.
Tip: If you notice improvements in your sleep and mood, acknowledge them. Small wins will motivate you to stay consistent with your new bedtime routine.

This plan is designed to be approachable and flexible, allowing you to set up lasting, positive habits.

Chapter 4

Tools and Techniques for Better Sleep

Mindfulness Practices for a Calmer Mind

Achieving better sleep often begins with calming the mind, especially if stress or mental chatter peaks as the day winds down. Mindfulness techniques such as deep breathing, visualization, and guided imagery can help set a peaceful tone, making it easier to drift off naturally.

Deep Breathing for Calm and Relaxation

Our breathing becomes shallow when we're tense or anxious, signalling stress to the body. Deep breathing helps counteract this by slowing down the heart rate, releasing muscle tension, and inviting a sense of calm. One popular method is the 4-7-8 technique: breathe in through your nose for a count of four, hold for seven, and exhale through your mouth for eight. Try repeating this for a few cycles to reset your nervous system.

If you're new to deep breathing, remember to keep it comfortable. It's not about forcing long breaths but about gently easing your mind and body into a state of relaxation. Consider placing one hand on your chest and the other on your belly for an added comfort layer. Feel the breath travel deep into your lungs and notice how, with each cycle, tension melts away.

Visualization: Creating Calm Through Imagery

Visualization is a powerful way to shift focus from the day's stresses to a more peaceful state. In a quiet space, close your eyes and imagine a place where you feel completely relaxed—a favorite natural spot, a cozy room, or even a simple, peaceful scene floating in calm water.

Picture the details: the sounds, the colors, the temperature. Each aspect you visualize helps deepen your relaxation and pulls you further from lingering stress.

For those who need a specific scene, imagine yourself in a warm field at dusk, where the air is still and comforting. Picture the sun setting slowly, casting a soft light across the sky. Let the scene draw you into a sense of calm with each breath.

Guided Imagery to Disconnect from Daytime Stresses

Guided imagery, or structured visualization, is similar to visualization but usually follows a mental "script" or an audio guide. Walking you through a calming scene often works while inviting you to relax each part of your body. Many find that guided imagery is particularly useful for sleep because it actively replaces stressful thoughts with a peaceful "story" the mind can focus on instead.

You can create a simple narrative if you don't have a guide. Start by mentally relaxing each part of your body—beginning with your toes, gradually moving upward until you reach the top of your head. Imagine a sense of warmth and heaviness spreading as you go, creating a deep sense of peace. This approach can help you overcome the day's challenges and prepare your mind for sleep.

Journaling for Sleep: Clearing Mental Clutter

Our minds are rarely blank at bedtime. Often, thoughts about what happened during the day or what's ahead tomorrow can keep us from winding down. Journaling offers a chance to empty these thoughts, clearing mental clutter and allowing you to end the day with a sense of closure.

Try a "brain dump" exercise where you jot down whatever is on your mind without editing or organizing. The goal here isn't perfect prose but to release your worries and ideas. You might find it helpful to create categories like "tasks for tomorrow" or "reflections on today." Writing them down can reassure you that everything is accounted for, and there's no need to keep thinking about it in bed.

Another helpful approach is gratitude journaling. Instead of focusing on tomorrow's to-do list, take a few minutes to note what went well today. This shift in focus can make a big difference, helping you fall asleep with positive thoughts rather than anxieties.

Optimizing Sleep with Sleep Hygiene Essentials

Good sleep hygiene is the foundation for restful nights. These habits and environment adjustments help signal your body that it's time for sleep, creating the ideal setting for quality rest.

The Importance of Consistent Sleep Schedules

Our bodies operate on circadian rhythms, or internal clocks, which thrive on consistency.

Going to bed and waking up at the same time every day—even on weekends—reinforces a natural sleep-wake cycle that makes it easier to fall asleep and wake up feeling refreshed.

Creating a consistent schedule may involve winding down earlier than usual, mainly if you've habitually stayed up late.

Start by shifting your bedtime back in small increments—about 15 minutes earlier every few days—until you reach your target time. Once you establish this rhythm, you'll likely find falling asleep easier and waking up without an alarm.

Temperature, Darkness, and Noise: Creating a Restful Space

Environmental factors like temperature, light, and sound can significantly influence sleep quality. Here are some adjustments to make your bedroom as conducive to sleep as possible

Temperature: Aim for a cool room, around 65°F (18°C), as the body naturally cools when preparing for sleep. If this isn't feasible, consider using a fan or adjusting the bedding layers to stay comfortable.

Darkness: Darkness signals the brain to release melatonin, a hormone essential for sleep. Try using blackout curtains or an eye mask to block out light. Avoid electronics close to bedtime, as the blue light from screens can disrupt melatonin production.

Noise: If you're sensitive to sound, white noise machines or apps can help mask disruptive noises, creating a steady background sound that soothes rather than startles. Consider a fan or a nature-inspired white noise track for a natural approach.

Tips for Managing Late-Night Anxiety and Overthinking

Sometimes, no matter how perfect the environment or routine, late-night anxiety and overthinking can creep in. Here are some practical ways to manage those racing thoughts and settle into a peaceful night's rest.

The "Worry Window": Set aside a specific time earlier in the evening for dealing with worries or planning. This "worry window" gives you a dedicated space to address concerns rather than taking them to bed with you. Once your worry window is over, remind yourself that these thoughts must wait until tomorrow.

Grounding Techniques: Grounding exercises, like the 5-4-3-2-1 technique, can help shift your focus from internal anxieties to the present moment. Identify five things you can see, four you can touch, three you can hear, two you can smell, and one you can taste (or imagine). This exercise pulls you into the sensory present, quieting the mind.

Mindful Breathing: If you notice your mind wandering back to worries, practice mindful breathing to anchor yourself. Breathing deeply

and slowly can signal to your brain that it's safe
to relax. With practice, this can become a
powerful tool to calm the mind and redirect your
focus toward restful sleep.

Chapter 5

Sustaining the Break-Up and Building Better Habits

Rewiring Your Brain for Digital Balance

The Science of Habit Formation and Long-Term Change

Breaking a habit woven into daily life—like checking the phone at every spare moment—requires patience and understanding. Our brains are wired to seek comfort, and familiar routines feel safe. But this process isn't fixed; it can be reshaped, thanks to the brain's "neuroplasticity," which allows it to form new pathways and adopt healthier habits.

When trying to build new patterns, it helps to think of your brain as a forest trail. The paths you walk are often the easiest to follow, while unused trails become overgrown and harder to access.

You're strengthening a new path when you resist the urge to check your phone before bed or choose a book over scrolling. Repeating these choices, especially when the urge to revert is strong, solidifies the new pattern, making the healthier habit the go-to option over time.

Starting with small steps encourages lasting change. That could mean powering down your phone 15 minutes earlier each night or leaving it outside the bedroom altogether.

The key is to repeat these actions consistently, allowing your brain to build and reinforce pathways that align with your goals for better sleep and more focus.

How to Avoid "Digital Relapse" and Sustain Your Progress

Staying on track can feel challenging once you've established healthier habits, especially during stressful moments when reaching for the phone seems like a comfort. But avoiding a "digital relapse" doesn't require drastic measures—just some preparation.

Recognize High-Risk Situations: Many people revert to old habits when tired, stressed, or bored. Identify these situations and be ready with simple alternatives. For example, if you're tempted to scroll through social media at night, keep a book, journal, or crossword puzzle by your bed. Having a substitute ready makes it easier to stick with your plan.

Set Boundaries with Technology: Defining personal rules around phone usage gives structure. This might mean setting limits on certain apps, disabling notifications during specific hours, or designating certain rooms in your home as phone-free. When these guidelines are clear, it's easier to keep phone use in check, avoiding unnecessary screen time.

Take Intentional Pauses: Before picking up your phone, pause and ask yourself if it's essential. If it's not urgent, challenge yourself to wait a few minutes before acting impulsively. This brief delay encourages mindfulness, helping you recognize the moments when reaching for your phone is just a habit, not a need.

Track Benefits Regularly: Reflecting on the positive changes from reduced screen time can reinforce your commitment. Keeping a simple log of your mood, sleep quality, or productivity offers a clear view of your progress. When temptation strikes, these reminders serve as motivation to keep going.

Creating a Personal Support System for Success

No one's journey to digital wellness has to be a solo mission. Sharing your goals with others adds layers of support, accountability, and even joy to the process. Here's how to create a supportive environment that keeps you on track:

Find an Accountability Partner: Partnering with a friend, family member, or coworker who shares similar goals can make a difference. Set up regular check-ins, whether a weekly coffee date or a quick text exchange, to celebrate progress and discuss challenges. Knowing someone is cheering you on—and vice versa—can motivate you to sustain new habits.

Share Your Goals with Loved Ones: Openly explaining your goals helps others understand your journey and offers an opportunity to ask for support. Tell close friends or family why you're cutting down on screen time and how they can help.

This might mean asking them not to send late-night texts or joining you in screen-free activities, like a phone-free family dinner.

Join a Community Focused on Digital Balance: Finding an online or in-person community focused on healthy tech use offers a sense of belonging and encouragement. Communities offer shared experiences, ideas, and tips to navigate the challenges of reducing screen time. Whether it's an online forum, a local meetup, or a digital wellness group, these spaces can be valuable sources of support.

Use Self-Encouragement as Reinforcement: Recognize and celebrate your successes along the way. Simple affirmations like, "I'm enjoying restful nights without screens," or "I feel more present each day" can reinforce your commitment. Positive self-talk reduces the likelihood of relapse by nurturing a sense of pride and accomplishment.

Morning Energy Boosts Without the Phone

Phone-Free Morning Routines for a Fresh Start

Mornings set the tone for the rest of the day. Starting without immediately reaching for a phone creates a calmer, more intentional beginning. Here are some simple, phone-free ways to ease into the day:

Enjoy a Quiet Breakfast: Start your morning with tea, coffee, or breakfast without screens. Let this time be one of quiet reflection or conversation with loved ones. Focus on the flavors, the warmth of your drink, and the calm of starting the day at your own pace. Without digital distractions, you'll likely notice a sense of calm that lingers through the morning.

Incorporate Movement: A little movement—whether stretching, a quick yoga session, or a short walk outdoors—invigorates the body and wakes the mind. Moving first thing in the morning sets a positive tone and encourages natural alertness, making facing the day with energy and focus easier.

Set Daily Intentions: Take a few minutes to decide what matters most today. Setting an intention can offer clarity and purpose, whether you jot down one goal or reflect quietly.

This small habit grounds the day, aligning your actions with what feels truly important rather than letting digital distractions dictate your focus.

Practice Mindful Breathing: A few deep breaths help reset the mind and body in the morning. You could practice a simple breathing exercise, like inhaling deeply, holding for a few seconds, and exhaling slowly. This quiet moment refreshes the mind, preparing you to tackle the day with calm and focus.

Quick Practices for Boosted Mood and Mental Clarity

Phone-free practices that take only a few minutes can enhance mood and sharpen focus. Here are several techniques to boost mental clarity throughout the day:

Stretch Breaks: Physical movement brings mental clarity. A quick stretch break relieves tension and refreshes the body. Even standing up, rolling your shoulders, or reaching for the sky can release tightness and lift your spirits.

Mindful Hydration: Staying hydrated keeps the mind clear and alert. Each time you reach for water, use it as a reminder to pause, breathe, and reset. This small habit promotes hydration and mindfulness, helping you stay focused without reaching for your phone.

Engage Your Senses: Reconnect with your senses when you start feeling scattered or stressed. Step outside, feel the breeze, listen to the sounds, or smell a fresh cup of tea. Engaging the senses grounds you in the present moment, naturally boosting mental clarity.

Mini-Reflection Sessions: At various points in the day, take a minute to reflect on how you feel and what you need. Ask yourself questions like, "What's my focus right now?" or "Am I using my time in a way that aligns with my goals?"

These quick check-ins can provide insights, helping you stay mindful and present.

Staying Connected to Your Intentions Throughout the Day

Keeping your goals at the forefront requires gentle reminders and small practices reinforcing your focus. Here's how to stay connected to your intentions throughout the day:

Use Visual Reminders: Placing a reminder where you'll see it often—a sticky note, a screensaver, or a personal object—keeps your goals in mind. A phrase like "Stay Present" or "Focus on Rest" can serve as a gentle nudge toward staying on track.

Plan Scheduled Screen Breaks: Taking scheduled pauses helps prevent mindless scrolling. Step away from screens periodically, whether for a few minutes to breathe or for a quick walk outside. These breaks refresh your mind and keep digital fatigue at bay, making it easier to stick with your goals.

Practice Single-Tasking: Multitasking can be exhausting and leads to digital overload. Focusing on one task at a time—whether reading, working, or cooking—brings a sense of calm and satisfaction. It's a small way to stay intentional and aligned with your goal of balanced screen time.

Reflect on Progress Each Evening: End the day with a brief reflection on your goals. Ask yourself, "Did I stay mindful today?" or "What felt balanced about my screen use?" This reflection helps you acknowledge progress and recognize areas to improve, creating a natural rhythm of awareness and adjustment.

Chapter 6

Enjoying the Benefits of Better Sleep

Experiencing Real Rest and Renewal

Imagine waking up in the morning feeling genuinely refreshed, with a lightness that follows you into the day. This kind of rest doesn't leave you reaching for coffee after coffee; instead, it's a feeling that sustains you through daily challenges and activities.

Quality sleep is more than just lying down for eight hours—it's about getting the rest that allows your body and mind to recover fully.

When you commit to nightly habits that reduce screen time and prioritize relaxation, your body responds incredibly. Your mind quiets, your heart rate slows, and your system knows it's safe to release the tension it holds. This level of rest goes beyond physical; it supports your mental clarity, helping you feel centered as you move through the day. Small changes in your sleep habits add up, and with time, you'll likely notice that morning drowsiness fades and your mind feels clear and ready for the day.

Tracking and Celebrating Your Progress

As you continue to improve your sleep habits, tracking your progress is a valuable way to stay motivated and engaged. A journal dedicated to sleep can become a powerful tool, allowing you to record how you feel each morning, note any adjustments to your routine, and recognize patterns in your sleep quality.

Celebrating progress might seem small, but it's essential to building long-lasting habits. Maybe after a week of consistent sleep, you reward yourself with something meaningful—a good book or a relaxing weekend outing.

These moments remind you that you're making tangible progress and reinforce the benefits of your efforts. Tracking also brings awareness to any challenges, helping you fine-tune your approach. Over time, these small celebrations create a positive feedback loop, helping you build a lifestyle that values rest and balance.

Unexpected Benefits: Creativity, Productivity, and Mood

One of the biggest surprises about improving sleep quality is its impact on creativity and productivity. Without the fog of sleep deprivation, your mind can explore ideas, make connections, and solve problems with new clarity. You may find yourself approaching tasks with fresh solutions and even experiencing breakthroughs in previously challenging areas.

A well-rested mind also means better focus, making staying engaged in work, personal projects, or hobbies easier. This enhanced focus often extends to improved emotional balance as well. Quality sleep helps regulate the mood by allowing the brain to process emotions more fully, leaving you more patient, resilient, and better equipped to handle stress. When you feel calm and productive, it's not just your tasks that benefit—your overall satisfaction with life grows, too.

How Quality Sleep Can Deepen Relationships

The ripple effects of good sleep reach into every area of your life, and relationships are no exception. When well-rested, you bring more presence and empathy into interactions with friends, family, and colleagues. Instead of reacting out of exhaustion or irritability, you have the patience to listen, engage, and respond thoughtfully.

Being present isn't just about showing up physically; it's about being mentally and emotionally there for the people around you.

The benefits of better sleep show up in small moments—a meaningful conversation, a shared laugh, or the simple joy of being with others. Over time, these moments strengthen your connections, helping you build deeper, more fulfilling relationships.

Becoming Your Sleep Advocate

Your commitment to better sleep is a commitment to yourself. As you progress on this path, becoming your own advocate is important. Prioritizing your sleep may mean setting boundaries with your phone, protecting your night time routines, or even communicating your sleep goals with those around you.

As your advocate, you'll learn to honor your needs by choosing habits that support your well-being. This might mean politely declining evening plans if you know it will interfere with your sleep or gently encouraging family members to keep distractions to a minimum in the evenings.

The more you practice self-advocacy, the easier it is to make choices that align with your goals.

Staying Committed to Your Health and Well-being

Maintaining these changes over time is not always easy, but staying committed keeps your health and well-being at the forefront. Establishing your sleep routine as a non-negotiable part of life can be incredibly empowering.

Each night, you give your body and mind the time they need to recover, knowing that this investment will pay off in the way you feel each day.

Staying committed also means showing compassion to yourself if you have occasional setbacks. On nights when you find yourself tempted to scroll or stay up late, take a moment to remind yourself of why you started this journey.

Every step you take toward consistent, quality sleep strengthens your foundation of well-being, giving you the energy and resilience to face whatever life brings.

Tools for Managing Future Tech Overload

In a world that's constantly "on," staying mindful of digital use is key to maintaining the progress you've made. Developing a set of go-to tools for managing tech overload will help you maintain balance. Apps that track screen time, reminders to take tech-free breaks, or a consistent "digital curfew" can make a big difference in how you feel daily.

Having these tools in place allows you to enjoy the benefits of technology without sacrificing your rest. For example, creating tech-free zones in your home, such as the bedroom or dining area, helps reduce unnecessary digital interactions.

By setting up boundaries in advance, you're giving yourself a head start on preserving the quality of your sleep and protecting your well-being.

Spreading the Word

Your progress can inspire those around you. Sharing your sleep journey, the changes you've noticed, and the steps you've taken can encourage friends and family to think about their sleep habits. Invite loved ones to join you in simple practices, like setting screen limits in the evening or trying a digital detox together for a weekend.

As others see the positive effects of sleep on your life, they may feel inspired to explore similar changes. Even small steps, like suggesting phone-free activities or sharing the benefits you've experienced, can have a ripple effect, fostering a community of support around better sleep and digital balance.

Conclusion

Your journey toward better sleep and digital balance is not just about breaking up with your phone—it's about welcoming a new chapter in your life, one where restful nights and energized days become the norm. The routines you've created and the insights you've gained form the foundation for this chapter, giving you the tools to thrive both at night and during the day.

Reflecting on Your Progress and Looking Ahead

Remember to acknowledge each step you've taken as you reflect on how far you've come. Whether you've reduced screen time, created a peaceful sleep environment, or set boundaries around technology, each change contributes to a healthier, more balanced life.

Looking ahead, you can continue adapting your habits and fine-tuning your approach, ensuring that restful nights remain a lasting part of your routine.

Embracing the Freedom of Better Sleep and Less Screen Time

With each passing day, you'll experience the freedom that comes with better sleep and a balanced relationship with technology. This freedom isn't just about getting more rest—it's about reclaiming your energy, focus, and quality of life. Without the pull of constant connectivity, you have more room to pursue the things that matter to you, bringing greater satisfaction to each part of your life.

Your New Path to Rest and Balance

This journey is not about perfection; it's about progress. Each step toward better sleep and balanced digital use is toward a healthier, happier you. You have the tools and the knowledge to protect your rest, prioritize your well-being, and navigate technology in a way that enhances your life, not detracts from it.

Embrace this new path, and enjoy the lasting rewards of a life grounded in rest and balance.